The Successful Student

Workbook

"Turning Knowledge into Results"

By

Patricia Orlunwo Ikiriko

The Successful Student Workbook

First published in 2015 by Patricia Orlunwo Ikiriko

www.patriciaikiriko.com

pikiriko@hotmail.com

This book is available online and in bookstores.

Dedication

This book is dedicated to my loving and caring husband Hon (Evang) Hope Odhuluma Ikiriko, and children Doxa Chiudushime and Chanan-Christie Ikiriko.

Legal Disclaimer

Praise for the book

Patricia Ikiriko does a thorough job in explaining clearly from first principles how to get into the right frame of mind for studying and the practical steps one should take to achieve one's goals, including tips about time management, self-belief, self-responsibility and learning styles.

Catherine O'Brien PhD

Cambridge University UK

I believe strongly that this book will mark a change in many lives.

Mrs Iberie Addey, Senior Business Consultant,

International Business Machines Corporation,

IBM United Kingdom (UK)

This book is primarily a study guide aimed at undergraduate students, students aspiring to gain admission into the tertiary institutions, and every major stakeholder who has vested interest in improving the academic achievement of the present generation.

It provides basic insight on some hidden psychological factors such as fear, anxiety, low self-esteem, poor self-efficacy and external locus of control which militate against students' academic achievement and proffers realistic techniques such as

SMARTS, BREAKS, and ACADEMIC SUCCESS

TIPS among others as relevant solutions to combat these

psychological maladies

Decision + Determination + Hard work = Distinction, is a great formulae of success to internalize.

Dr Chinelo Ugwu, Counselling Psychologist,
University of Port Harcourt, Nigeria

I found this book very interesting, up to date and informative. It is very beneficial especially for all formal learners and teachers in a learning process and career planning. It discusses internal and external factors that affect a learning process and their solution. It also develops confidence in students to achieve their goals. At least it encourages me in my studies.

Sadia Aleem, University of Bedfordshire,
Department of Psychology Research Student,
LU1 3JU, UK

This book is a "must-read" for everyone desiring to be successful at whatever they choose to do - (be it learning, studying or accomplishing any given tasks) because of the practical tips and life changing techniques it provides at every chapter.

Eric I. Ekwe, BSc (Hons); MBA; PGD; MSc - Tech Mgmt.
CASSIDIAN

So many things I thought 'I cannot do' become 'things I might be able to do'. I believe that taking responsibility for your learning, after reading this wonderful book, cannot be very difficult anymore!!

This book provided necessary background information and offered solutions to replace bad study habits and apply the new one to the real world.

Only six steps between moving from your drawbacks old habits to the outstanding new habits ... Find them now inside this book!!

Saleh Alkhathami,

University of Bedfordshire Department of Psychology Research Student

This book is an invaluable aid because it is simple, easy to read and practical. It tells you not only 'what' to do but 'how' to excel as a student.

Gbenga Apampa

Vice President (Sustainable Development)

TOTAL Head Office. Paris. France

Workbook Overview

This workbook is intended to be used in conjunction with the main book "The Successful Student" by the same author published by Panoma Press..

There are three key elements in this workbook:

- My personal reflection – insight gained in each chapter
- Key concepts – points to remember
- Exercises – action learning system

My personal reflection- gained insight

To attain educational success: "Always keep the big picture of studying in mind". The personal reflection is designed to help you do just that. The first aim when studying is to have a grasp of the real background of the topic, and how you can easily remember it frequently.

The personal reflection is a guide to keep you to your commitment to academic excellence. Remember, it is your action (inaction) that will decide between success and failure in achieving good educational result.

Every time you complete a topic, allow yourself to reflect on the core insight gained. This simple activity rewards your subconscious mind and encourages you on to retain information studied.

Key concepts learned

Remembering your learning experiences is one of the most powerful motivational tools that create knowledge and insight for you to draw on for future reference. The key learning concept system is about learning by studying, taking action, reviewing the content in detail, and writing down your key learning points. But, note your challenges with your study habits skills and further learning needed. Check how quickly and thoroughly you have adapted to right study style and methods for better educational performance.

Exercises

This is where your brain meets with blueprint to educational success, and where you get the chance to transform learning into result.

With each action step, you will find the purpose of that step and "tips" to help you complete it effectively. At the end of the question, there is space for you to record your activity, and summarize your key learning points.

Contents

Introduction

Welcome to the successful student action plan and guide to academic success.

The workbook is carefully designed to give you all the time and attention you need to develop important basic knowledge of attaining educational goals. I want you to succeed. I failed in school and have seen countless people fail, through impatience, lack of knowledge, and of not knowing how to study and learn effectively.

Aims

The aim of this workbook is to empower students to develop the ability to organize themselves, their time, their work and turning knowledge gained in studying into reality (educational excellence). Writing down key ideas when studying helps you retain valuable insights that would slip away with daily pressure. Cognitive and educational psychologists say that handwriting has unique cognitive properties that elicit motor activity in the brain and help to shape how children learn to read.

The objective is to provide you with:
- A record for future retrieval;
- To reinforce your memory;

- To strengthen your personal involvement with the materials learned;
- To capture and keep the treasure of learning that is discovered in the progression of studying;
- To attract the perfect opportunities to make the progress you desire; and
- Reinforce your sense of fulfillment

Your Personal Goal Setting

Develop a personal goal programme to keep you accountable to your commitment and encourage you in identifying your specific interest in studying the subject. Completing each exercise will give energy and focus to your learning process.

Example:

A brief description of what you want in real term that is passionate to you, as if it were already achieved

8 STEPS TOWARDS YOUR GOAL SETTING

1. Decide exactly what you want to achieve and write it out simply.

2. Determine steps to overcome obstacles.

3. Define the skills you need to acquire.

4. Decide on the company to keep

5. Set a deadline.

6. Make detailed plans to achieve your goals.

7. Take action.

8. Believe in yourself

Action

Weekly action steps

Monday	
Tuesday	
Wednesday	
Thursday	
Friday	
Saturday	
Sunday	

Chapter 1: Studying

Personal Reflection

-PATRICIA IKIRIKO

What was the biggest "Aha" moment or insight you gained from this chapter?

_____

_____

_____

_____

What are your STRENGTHS in the area of Studying?

_____

_____

_____

_____

What are your WEAKNESSES in the area of Studying?

_____

_____

_____

_____

Where are your OPPORTUNITES to grow in the area of Studying?

_____

_____

_____

What are the THREATS to your growth in the area of studying?

_____

_____

_____

_____

Key Concepts

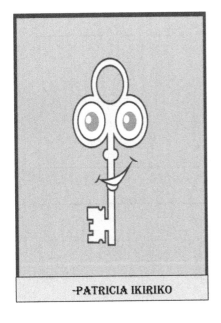

-PATRICIA IKIRIKO

1. What is "unconscious incompetence"?

_____

_____

_____

_____

2. Give an example of when you have experienced
    "unconscious incompetence" in your life.

_____

_____

_____

_____

3. What is "conscious incompetence"?

_____

_____

_____

_____

4. Give an example of when you have experienced "conscious incompetence" in your life.

_____

_____

_____

_____

5. What is "conscious competence"?

_____

_____

_____

_____

6. Give an example of when you have experienced "conscious incompetence" in your life.

_____

_____

_____

_____

7. What is "unconscious competence"?

_____

_____

_____

_____

8. Give an example of when you have experienced
    "unconscious incompetence" in your life.

_____

_____

_____

_____

Time for Exercise

-PATRICIA IKIRIKO

Think about how you currently apply yourself to studying.

What are your habits?

How successful are they?

With regard to your current ability to study productively and learn actively, where do you currently sit with regard to the four stages of learning that we discussed above?

Chapter 2: Understanding student attitudes

You can't get a rainbow

if you're looking down

What was the biggest "Aha" moment or insight you gained from this chapter?

_____

_____

_____

_____

What are your **STRENGTHS** in your attitude to work?

_____

_____

_____

_____

What are your **WEAKNESSES** in your attitude to work?

_____

_____

_____

_____

Where are your **OPPORTUNITIES** to improve your attitude?

_____

_____

_____

_____

What are the **THREATS** to improving your attitude?

_____

_____

_____

_____

Key Concepts

-PATRICIA IKIRIKO

1. What is "failure"?

Give an example of when you have experienced "failure" in your life.

_____

_____

_____

_____

2. What is "determination"?

Give an example of when you have experienced "determination" in your life.

_____

_____

_____

_____

3. What is "anxiety"?

Give an example of when you have experienced "anxiety" in your life.

_____

_____

_____

_____

4. What is "fear"?

Give an example of when you have experienced "fear" in your life.

_____

_____

_____

Time for Exercise

-PATRICIA IKIRIKO

Almost everyone has room for improvement in some area of their life, whether due to unrealistic expectations, faulty thinking due to previous poor experiences, or an incorrect belief that something is subject to an external locus of control (LOC) and therefore outside of their control.

Write out habits holding you back

List 5 steps to change bad habits and explain how you can make decision to change them

Chapter 3: Offering support to individual students

-PATRICIA IKIRIKO

What was the biggest "Aha" moment or insight you gained from this chapter?

_____

_____

_____

_____

How **RESPONSIBLE** are you when it comes to your work?

_____

_____

_____

_____

What **OPPORTUNITIES** do you have to improve your
RESPONSIBILITY?

_____

_____

_____

_____

What **THREATS** are there for you trying to improve your
RESPONSIBILITY?

_____

_____

_____

The Three stepping stones of success

-PATRICIA IKIRIKO

1.   Why are you doing what you're doing?

Give an example of how you can identify your core motivation in what you're doing.

_____

_____

_____

_____

2.   What are you doing to support what you want to do?

Give an example of the steps you've put in place to help you attain your goals

_____

_____

_____

_____

3.   Who are your mentors?

Give an example of your established support system that helps you as you go.

_____

_____

_____

_____

-PATRICIA IKIRIKO

1. What is "success"?

Give an example of when you have experienced "success" in your life.

What strategic step-by-step approach, are you taking to get organised and take full charge of your situation?

_____

_____

_____

_____

2. What is "overachieving ambition"?

Give an example of when you have experienced "overachieving ambition" in your life.

_____

_____

_____

_____

3. What is "anxiety"?

Give an example of when you have experienced "anxiety" in your life.

_____

_____

_____

_____

4. What is "fear"?

Give an example of when you have experienced "fear" in your life.

_____

_____

_____

_____

Time for Exercise

-PATRICIA IKIRIKO

What is your overarching goal?

Start by asking yourself the following questions:

- What would give my life true meaning and value?

- What would enable me to feel satisfied with what I have achieved at the end of each day?

- What would allow me to approach each new day with a very real sense of purpose?

Take some time to think carefully about this; this is what you will be working hard over the next several years to achieve, so make sure you fully understand why you are doing it, and what is in it for you. Over time your list is likely to evolve and become more refined, and you will find that a clearer picture begins to emerge. Keep your list safe and look at it regularly; this will help you to maintain your focus and commitment.

What's most important to you?

Is what you are doing the right way to go about achieving your overarching ambition?

Set realistic goals + Take steps to move towards them daily.

Chapter 4: Organizing and Managing your studies

-PATRICIA IKIRIKO

What was the biggest "Aha" moment or insight you gained from this chapter?

_____

_____

_____

_____

How **RESPONSIBLE** are you when it comes to **organizing your time well**?

Give an example of how you organize your time daily.

_____

_____

_____

_____

How **IRRESPONSIBLE** are you when it comes to **organizing your time well**?

_____

_____

_____

_____

What **OPPORTUNITIES** do you have to improve your **organization of time**?

_____

_____

_____

_____

What **THREATS** are there to you trying to improve your **organization of time**?

_____

_____

_____

_____

Key Concepts

-PATRICIA IKIRIKO

Major Threats to Educational Success

1. What is "Procrastination"?

Give an example of when you "procrastinated" in your studies.

_____

_____

_____

_____

2. What is "multitasking"?

Give a reason of why you might have to "multitask" in your studies.

_____

_____

_____

_____

3. What is "distraction"?

Give an example of when you have experienced a "distraction" in your studies.

_____

_____

_____

_____

4. What is "absent-mindedness"?

Give an example of when you have experienced "absent-mindedness" during working times.

_____

_____

_____

_____

5. What is the "80/20 rule"?

Give an example of how you intend to apply the "80/20 rule" in your studies

_____

_____

_____

_____

N.B- Given the overwhelming evidence of the detrimental effects of multitasking on studying and learning, YOU should practice focusing on one task until completion rather than doing many things simultaneously.

Time for Exercise

-PATRICIA IKIRIKO

How can you make a start by ensuring that your workspace is clear, tidy and well-equipped?

| |
| |
| |
| |
| |
| |

How would you accommodate your responsibilities to achieve your academic goals?

| |
| |
| |
| |
| |
| |

Hard work aligns you for excellence + Follow your To Do List.

Chapter 5: How to excel by using the right techniques

What was the biggest "Aha" moment or insight you gained from this chapter?

_____

_____

_____

_____

How **RESPONSIBLE** are you when it comes to **finding the right techniques**?

_____

_____

_____

_____

What **OPPORTUNITIES** do you have to improve your **techniques for work**?

_____

_____

_____

_____

What **THREATS** do you face when you're trying to improve you **techniques for work**?

_____

_____

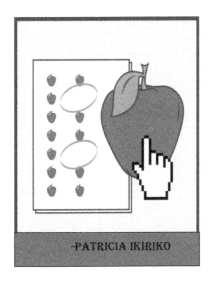

-PATRICIA IKIRIKO

Three types of Learning Techniques

- Setting SMART objectives

- Using Gantt charts

- Using dynamic 'to do' lists.

1. What is a "Mnemonic"?

Give an example of when you would use "mnemonic" in your life.

_____

_____

_____

_____

2. What is "affirmation"?

Give an example of how you can use "affirmations" to change routines when getting more work done.

_____

_____

_____

_____

3. What is "time-framing"?

Give an example of how you can use "time-framing" to your advantage when improving your work.

_____

_____

_____

_____

4. What is a "deadline"?

Give an example of how effective a "deadline" is when working.

_____

_____

_____

_____

Time for Exercise

-PATRICIA IKIRIKO

Consider the two techniques described in the 'Maximizing time' section above: time-framing and waking early. How can you use time-framing to your advantage?

How would you benefit from effectively lengthening your day by either getting up earlier or going to bed later?

If you feel you can extend your day, make a plan as to how you will tackle the change (whether incrementally or in one fell swoop) and commit to its implementation. Make sure you use your extra time wisely! Write out your plan schedule:

Identify what works for you + Practice taking responsibility.

Chapter 6: Developing the right study Method for you

-PATRICIA IKIRIKO

What was the biggest "Aha" moment or insight you gained from this chapter?

_____

_____

_____

_____

How **RESPONSIBLE** are you when it comes to **finding the right study method**?

_____

_____

_____

_____

What **OPPORTUNITIES** do you have to improve your **study method**?

_____

_____

_____

_____

What **THREATS** are there to you trying to improve your **study method**?

_____

_____

_____

_____

The Learning Cycle

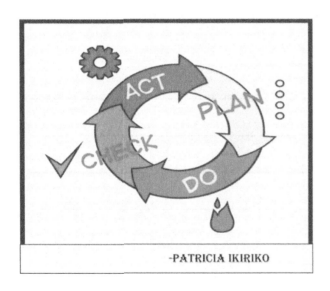

-PATRICIA IKIRIKO

Plan- Going through notes, setting aside time for homework, attending regular study groups

Do- Begin learning experience.

Check- Review what we've learnt using notes and asking others.

Act- Assess what is needed to do next

List the different styles of learning.

Describe the learning style that is most effective to you.

_____

_____

_____

_____

List the different strategies of note taking

_____

_____

_____

_____

List the Patricia Ikiriko techniques of studying and in your own words give examples of how you can apply it in your own studies.

_____

_____

_____

_____

   **Key Concepts**

1. What is "intuitive learning"?

Give an example of when you have experienced "intuitive learning" in your life?

_____

_____

_____

_____

2. What is "incidental learning"?

Give an example of when you have experienced "incidental learning in your life"?

_____

_____

_____

_____

3.   What is "retrospective learning"?

Give an example of when you have experienced "retrospective learning" in your life.

_____

_____

_____

_____

4.   What is "prospective learning"?

Give an example of when you have experienced "prospective learning" in your life.

_____

_____

_____

_____

Time for Exercise

-PATRICIA IKIRIKO

How can you practice using the BREAKS technique when studying?

When structuring information for recall, what can you bear in mind?

Follow the best learning techniques suitable for you + Practice to attain academic excellence.

Chapter 7: The best way to read a book

-PATRICIA IKIRIKO

What was the biggest "Aha" moment or insight you gained from this chapter?

_____

_____

_____

_____

How **RESPONSIBLE** are you when it comes to **reading effectively**?

_____

_____

_____

_____

What **OPPORTUNITIES** do you have to improve the effectiveness of your **reading**?

_____

_____

_____

_____

What **THREATS** are there to you trying to improve the effectiveness of your **reading**?

_____

_____

_____

_____

The Five Levels of Reading

-PATRICIA IKIRIKO

1. What is "preview reading"?

Give an example of when you have applied "preview reading" in your work?

_____

_____

_____

_____

2. What is "inspectional reading"?

Give an example of when you have applied "inspectional reading" when doing homework?

_____

_____

_____

_____

3. What is "elementary reading"?

Give an example of when you have applied"elementary reading" in your work.

_____

_____

_____

_____

4. What is "analytical reading"?

Give an example of when you have applied "analytical reading" while you're working.

_____

_____

_____

_____

5. What is "syntopical reading"?

Give an example of when you have applied "syntopical reading" when doing work.

_____

_____

_____

_____

Time for Exercise

-PATRICIA IKIRIKO

What are the processes of reading a book?

Can you explain to your classmate the four vital points to remember when reading a book?

In your own words write details on the best way to read a book?

Prepare, organize, and practice the techniques outlined here in order to get the most from your reading experiences.

Chapter 8: Good guide to different referencing styles

What was the biggest "Aha" moment or insight you gained from this chapter?

_____

_____

_____

_____

How **RESPONSIBLE** are you when it comes to **using references**?

_____

_____

_____

_____

What **OPPORTUNITIES** do you have to improve your **use of references**?

_____

_____

_____

_____

What **THREATS** are there to you trying to improve your **use of references**?

_____

_____

_____

_____

Key Concepts

-PATRICIA IKIRIKO

1. What is "referencing"?

Give an example of when you have used of "referencing" in your life?

_____

_____

_____

_____

2. Give an example of where you would use a reference?

_____

_____

_____

_____

3. Give an example of a referencing style.

_____

_____

_____

_____

4. Give an example of how you make notes of your references as you work along.

_____

_____

_____

_____

5. Give an example of your preferred referencing style.

_____

_____

_____

_____

The Four most commonly used styles of referencing

1.   Harvard;

2.   Modern Language Association America (MLA);

3.   Modern   Humanities   Research   Association (MHRA);

4.   British Numeric.

Time for Exercise

-PATRICIA IKIRIKO

Obtain a copy of your school referencing style guide. Read it and ensure you thoroughly understand it.

If anything is unclear, then you should either: Where would you go to clarify any issues?

| |
| |
| |
| |
| |
| |

How would you approach your tutor if you're unclear about your
work?

**N.B. If you are unable to obtain clarity by following step 1,
proceed to step 2.**

Get into the habit of organizing your references as you go along.

Chapter 9: How to research and source material for academic writing

-PATRICIA IKIRIKO

What was the biggest "Aha" moment or insight you gained from this chapter?

_____

_____

_____

_____

What are your **STRENGTHS** when it comes to your research for writing?

_____

_____

_____

_____

What are your **WEAKNESSES** when it comes to your research for writing?

_____

_____

_____

_____

Where are your **OPPORTUNITIES** to improve your research for writing?

_____

_____

_____

_____

What are the **THREATS** to improve your research for writing?

_____

_____

_____

_____

Key Concepts

-PATRICIA IKIRIKO

1. Give an example of when you would use a "scholarly journal" to improve your research when writing.

_____

_____

_____

_____

2. Give an example of when you have applied "signposting" to improve your research when writing.

_____

_____

_____

_____

3. Give an example of when you have used "newspapers" to improve your research when writing.

_____

_____

_____

_____

4. Give an example of when you have used "library services" to improve your research when writing.

_____

_____

_____

_____

Time for Exercise

-PATRICIA IKIRIKO

Exercise

Consider what would be the best regular sources of research for you (we're considering general rather than specialist sources here). Make a list of those places it would be appropriate to seek information, and in what order, and make this standard practice to kick-start your research each time you embark on a new topic.

Explain in your own words why researching is desirable?

List different areas you can get information from when researching?

Chapter 10: Academic Success Tips

-PATRICIA IKIRIKO

What was the biggest "Aha" moment or insight you gained from this chapter?

_____

_____

_____

_____

What are your **STRENGTHS** when it comes to focusing on your studies?

_____

_____

_____

_____

What are your **WEAKNESSES** when it comes to seeking information when studying?

_____

_____

_____

_____

Where are your **OPPORTUNITIES** to improve your approach to working?

_____

_____

_____

_____

Seven tips to educational excellence

1. Prepare before class

2. Always attend class

3. Master the skill of useful note taking

4. Make use of the library

5. Surround yourself with committed learners

6. Ask for help if you need it

7. Prepare for examinations

Exercise

-PATRICIA IKIRIKO

In your own words say how you can explain 10 methods you will put in place to achieve academic excellence.

In your own words how can you relate with your friends during a discussion to help with your work?

If you are really serious about being the best and moving to the top of your field, you cannot afford to spend your time with people who are going nowhere in their lives, no matter how nice they are. In this sense, you must be perfectly selfish with regard to yourself and your future ambitions. You must set high standards on your friends and associates and refuse to compromise. '- Brian Tracy

26 Vital points for improving yourself

A – Avoid stress, and keep focus to achieve your goal

B – Believe in yourself, mobilizing your strength, improving your weakness

C – Consider your goals carefully; be courageous despite tremendous doubt, moving towards mastery

D – Don't give in to discouragement; awareness of self is attaining self- mastery

E – Enjoy your work. Don't see the work before you as a big task eliminate poor time use by focusing on one thing at a time so you can get more done

F – Familiarize yourself with new concepts, appreciate yourself and be self-assured that you can do it

G – Give priority to your work, yourself, and play, and avoid distraction

H – Hold on to your dream of success, constantly improving your idea of self

I – Ignore any distracting factors. Idealize the kind of life you desire, and keep moving towards attaining your goals

J – Justify your friendships. Eliminate those that drag you off from your vision. Choose good friends that will encourage you to accomplish your vision.

K – Keep moving forward and don't be weary from obstacles before you, Instead, use the obstacles as stepping stone to greatness

L – Learn more from experts in your field; maintain positive attitude

M – Motivate yourself, be confident, and develop positive expectation, believing that things will turn out well in the end

N – Never feel shy when you need help

O – Open your mind to accept criticism; learn from each one, it's a helpful tool to make you a better person

P – Perfect practice makes perfect, learn to make things happen

Q – Quitters never win; winners never quit. Stay in the game until you win

R – Ready yourself, read, prepare carefully to win your prize

S – Stop procrastinating. It's a quick killer of progress

T – Take action early, and take control step by step; follow a MAP (Mind-set, Action, and Process) to win at life

U – Understand your strengths and weaknesses; utilize every opportunity to maximize your time

V – Visualize your desired end result and aim to achieve it by taking action and never make excuses

W – Wishing wouldn't achieve it, taking effective action will help make your dream a reality

X – X-factor is a programme you can watch for relaxation

Y – You have great potential within, your self-belief is very important to achieving your goals. You are unique

Z – Zip your mouth and talk less on every issue. Concentrate on your dream until you win.

Conclusion

The above action plan and guide establishes the fundamentals, and provides a powerful action plan that will enable you to get a good grade at school. Following the exercises diligently and consistently for sufficient time can lead you to achieve your educational goals.

Apply this action learning system by starting one chapter at a time, focus, and mastering the chapter to retain information accurately will help you:

- Have greater self-confidence;
- To gather insights and knowledge from the topics which will enrich your activities within the topic; and
- Be better prepared to improve your study habits and examination outcome.

The golden key

The master Key is to repeat, repeat, and repeat your reading to fully instill the new knowledge to become more productive and manage your time effectively to achieve your desired success.

References

Tracy, B. (2009) Flight plan the real secret of success. Berrett-Koehler Publisher Inc.

Ikiriko, P. O. (2013). The successful student. London: Panoma Press

About the author

Patricia Orlunwo Ikiriko is a counselling psychologist who has worked with different organizations involving young people for over 18 years. She is happily married to Hon. Hope Odhuluma Ikiriko and a mother blessed with two children, two foster children and a granddaughter.

She holds a Master of Philosophy in Psychology from the University of Bedfordshire, United Kingdom; Graduate Diploma in Psychology from the University Of East London, United Kingdom; a Master's degree in Education Guidance and Counselling from the University of Port Harcourt Rivers State Nigeria, a B.Ed. in Guidance, Counselling and Psychology from University Of Ibadan, Nigeria; and a National Certificate in Education from the University Of Ibadan, Nigeria.

She is a professional member of the British Psychology Society, the American Counseling Association, Counselling Association of Nigeria and a Doctoral candidate in Psychology.

She is involved in various youth programmes at the Redeemed Christian Church of God - Chapel of Glory International (RCCG-COGI), a non-profit organization in Watford, Hertfordshire, United Kingdom.

Patricia has a passion in helping young people to discover their unique and hidden potential, and encouraging them to fulfil their destiny in order to determine exactly who they are and what they want by setting clear, measurable, and achievable goals. She helps them to create a strategic plan as a sign-post to their desired destination and develop confidence in themselves, along with the qualities of endurance, persistence, and determination to remain focused on accomplishing their dream.

Her wealth of experience of working with young people in schools and different organizations for over 18 years has been an inspiration to her. She is currently conducting a research on the influence of parental involvement, teacher attitudes and counselling intervention on Nigerian senior Secondary students' study habits, locus of control and educational performance.

In addition, she is working with young people in schools and organisation involve in working with youth on a new programme titled "Young and Influential" developing leadership and wealth building skills in youth. A practical model for translating vision into reality building self-confidence in youth and assisting them translating vision into reality as well as strategies to create wealth

Her aim is to recommend strategies to help people understand and develop effective approaches to studying. She believes the best medium for reaching young people and accomplishing these goals would be through a book, using simple illustrative and accessible ways, which will convey key ideas and information to today's students.

This workbook is intended for use with "The Successful Student", by the same author and published by Panoma Press. "The Successful Student" is available online and in bookstores, ISBN 978-1-909623-18-7.

Made in the USA
Middletown, DE
04 March 2023

26153686R00056